T0068190

# FEED MY SHEEP, THEY ARE DYING

Transform leaders from general and
spiritual leaders to servant leader

DR. SHIRLEY A. YOUNG

WESTBOW
PRESS®
A DIVISION OF THOMAS NELSON
& ZONDERVAN

Scripture taken from the Holy Bible, NEW INTERNATIONAL VERSION®.
Copyright © 1973, 1978, 1984 by Biblica, Inc. All rights reserved worldwide.
Used by permission. NEW INTERNATIONAL VERSION® and NIV® are
registered trademarks of Biblica, Inc. Use of either trademark for the offering
of goods or services requires the prior written consent of Biblica US, Inc.

Scripture quotations taken from the Holy Bible, New Living Translation,
Copyright © 1996, 2004. Used by permission of Tyndale House
Publishers, Inc., Wheaton, Illinois 60189. All rights reserved.

WestBow Press books may be ordered through booksellers or by contacting:

WestBow Press
A Division of Thomas Nelson & Zondervan
1663 Liberty Drive
Bloomington, IN 47403
www.westbowpress.com
1 (866) 928-1240

Because of the dynamic nature of the Internet, any web addresses or
links contained in this book may have changed since publication and
may no longer be valid. The views expressed in this work are solely those
of the author and do not necessarily reflect the views of the publisher,
and the publisher hereby disclaims any responsibility for them.

Any people depicted in stock imagery provided by Thinkstock are
models, and such images are being used for illustrative purposes only.
Certain stock imagery © Thinkstock.

ISBN: 978-1-5127-2561-2 (sc)
ISBN: 978-1-5127-2562-9 (e)

Library of Congress Control Number: 2015921403

Print information available on the last page.

WestBow Press rev. date: 12/29/2015

# Contents

# Acknowledgements

My deepest gratitude goes to God for his provisions and spiritual encouragement to pursue doctoral studies despite the struggles and responding obediently gave rich knowledge.

Additionally, I want to thank the entire staff of Argosy University for their excellent assistance on the journey during 2012-14 based in part to Drs. Tom Kemp and Anne Nelson for their tireless counsel and direction in encouraging and guiding me to succeed.

Finally, thanks to my sons, extended family, clergy, ministry colleagues and friends for giving me much needed support over the past 4 years of the journey.

# Dedication

I dedicate my doctoral degree to my Lord and Savior Jesus Christ. It was His command and his presence that provided me the encouragement to fulfill my goal and succeed. God knew His servant's ability and obedience to fulfill the assignment to improve leaders in faith-based organizations.

Additionally, I dedicate my work posthumorously to my parents, James and Anna McNeely, who both inspired me, their eldest daughter, to achieve a doctoral. Notably, my maternal grandmother, Hester Silver Jenkins Lamb, was an English professor whose example helped me aspire for my highest level of achievement. Additionally, throughout my educational journey, Iska Alter, Professor Emeriti of English at Hofstra University in Garden City, N.Y. gave me encouragement.

During my master studies, I met Katie Geneva Cannon, Professor of Christian Ethics at Presbyterian School of Christian Education in Richmond, Virginia. Dr. Cannon's encouraging words "nothing is impossible with God" persevere to aspire to the highest achievement.

*Therefore, go and make disciples of all the nations, baptizing them in the name of the Father and the Son and the Holy Spirit. Teach these new disciples to obey all the commands I have given you. And be sure of this: I am with you always, even to the end of age. (Matthew 28:19-20, NLT), Bible Gateway*

# Introduction

The biblical verse captured this author's attention observing the concern that leaders are not recognizing discipleship teaching for growth of disciples is a priority for faith-based organizations (FBOs). The new millennium presents the opportunity to impart the experiential years of significance for Christian education since completing seminarian and doctoral studies. Discipleship growth through Christian education within the Protestant faith should be foundational for the people of God to benefit knowledge through teaching. Upon retirement, transitioning in 1998 to Hampton, Virginia joining a FBO gave reflection of a plunge in perspicacity continuous Christian pedagogy was foundational for discipleship growth. It was exciting finding a teaching/preaching protestant faith organization for continuous spiritual growth. Since transitioning in 1998, it is revelatory that clergy formerly Sunday schoolteachers are extending sermon messages into Sunday school scheduled time refuting sessions for Sunday school. Inquiry from clergy of former status why sermon messages are extensive, causing Sunday school to become obsolete, gave no tangible response. A lifetime Sunday school student growing through her spiritual journey feels dishearten while witnessing the dissipation of Sunday school in the 21$^{st}$ century. The biblical text of Matthew 28:19-20 sent my antennas up, wondering if clergy remember the words of Christ prior to his departure giving the command to all disciples of their responsibility to reach and teach.

The text became continuously audible while hearing the voice of God to pursue additional knowledge.

In 2000, obeying God's command to attend seminary achieving in 2006 the Master Degree for Christian Education inclusive of two seminaries. In 2007, regretfully God spoke again commanding this author to pursue studies for leadership concerns for FBOs. The years of 2007 and 2008 began the struggle of hearing God's voice, responding to research why leaders were affecting their followers exhibiting traumatic behaviors. Upon presenting the assumption at the time of dissertation, the professor gave declination to choose another topic specifically servant leader and not general leadership behaviors.

21st Century leaders began exhibiting immoral and unethical behaviors with attitudes affecting their integrity causing extinction of FBOs from leaders not influencing the image of Christ to followers. Since transitioning from northern culture to southern culture, it became obvious there is a plummet in discipleship teaching that is dispiriting. Matthew 28:19-20 became extant during the research for leadership concern relative to Robert Greenleaf's 1970 study of students' revolt versus university employees lacking character traits with incompetency. Further communication with the professor in preparation for research was focusing towards Greenleaf's study reflecting support of introducing his ten character traits for leadership transformation. Greenleaf's resource became recommendable for transforming leaders of profit and nonprofit faith-based organizations with new leadership constructs. The research did accomplish a successful statistical analysis using cooperative participants determining if leaders were affecting their followers with behaviors and attitudes using a leadership survey. Research results were astonishing recognizing FBOs require new leadership constructs to grant the opportunity to consider transformation through teaching and training. Again, Matthew 28:19-20 would continue to become visible in my mind giving clarity for the research theory, specifically the probability that leaders are not all "called" by God causing disparity in ministry.

Observations of FBO senior clergy leaders are selecting secular leaders, not revering the spiritual "call" servants that could influence Christ. Christian education in FBOs is obsolete failing to teach moral behaviors and attitudes. The objective for senior "shepherds" of faith-based organizations should be for disciples to receive Christian education. The education teaches images of Christ for disciples to characterize traits/standards to become servants with leadership growth. The text of Matthew 28:19-20 states God expects leaders to obey His command to commit, to baptize and teach far as they will go having his spiritual presence always with each disciple. Responding obediently to pursue further studies was assuming a problem did exist with leaders in FBOs compromising loss of integrity, trust, and confidence in leaders, lacking successful organizations with disruption of leader's gifts.

Leadership development with teaching and training from Christian education currently is administratively redundant in FBOs in the southern and northern culture assuming to be nationwide. The redundancy is reflective through clergy believing their sermons, bible study is sufficient Christian education for the body of believers with revival messages and other visiting messengers. If leaders would meditate, revisit the first seven years of childhood, they would learn those years gave traumatic occurrences in the life of every living creature requiring healing, strength, and development to become a servant for God. Unfortunately, the foundation of teaching according to Matthew 28 is the key to spiritual development that someone should alert FBOs to resume. Of course, recommendation of research could determine if it is denominational by leadership and not an ecclesiastical change of law.

The resource introduce new constructs for educators, senior clergy and ministry leaders to evaluate self and subordinate leaders for transformation: (a) evaluate self determining type of FBO leader that view values to develop changes, (b) teach FBO organizational leaders to emulate character traits of Christ the ultimate servant leader.

It is possible to combine traits with ethical values, appropriate leadership styles for FBO leaders to influence society positively to overcome negativity. The research was able to uncover and identify weak characteristic traits of behaviors and attitudes toward followers within FBO's that require improving for effective leadership. The 21$^{st}$ century affords the opportunity to introduce new resources for the faith-based organizations (FBOs) leadership ministry. It is an invaluable opportunity to encourage disciples of FBOs how to expand their horizons during the 21$^{st}$ century.

There are questions: Do you know your identity in Christ? Do you know your spiritual gift that God gives to each disciple? Are you a leader or servant leader? Are you receiving discipleship teaching with training in your FBO?

The author's background encompasses the blend of northern and southern cultures of spiritual experiences for teaching and training disciples for kingdom building. Since transitioning to the southern culture in 1998, this author became aware of revolt in spiritual structure of FBOs leadership ministry. Leadership is about people, with displeasure of the existing Christian education revolt disturbing the author recognizing it is probably nationwide. Disqualifying Christian pedagogy, leaders of ministries affects followers' especially new disciples not receiving teaching or training that should be foundational for FBOs as the former experience. An author, teacher, and servant of Christian education there is keen awareness of discontinuance discipleship teaching in FBOs. Matthew 28:19-20 is a key message saying the Holy Spirit moves like a mighty, rushing wind and it shall resume teaching for disciples to develop a relationship with the Father and Son.

God chooses Christian educators with a "calling" and leaders selecting secular teachers are unable to hear God's voice for direction. Therefore, FBOs would be acquiescent for the author's publication of transforming leaders to servant leaders exhibiting 'traits and standards. Leadership is a daunting task when micromanaging secular leaders. The "uncalled" senior leaders might be lacking spiritual discernment assuming they are to micromanage subordinate leaders that God "calls". Spiritual discernment is a gift God gives to selective "called" servants that hear specific instructions from God as "uncalled" without discernment are unable to hear God's directives.

The challenge for leadership ministry in the FBOs is introducing new constructs of traits and standards to transform leaders to servant leader's that derives from a research manuscript by this author. Leadership influences society, corporate America and faith-based organizations. Resource for corporate America will be a future publication as organizations faces extinction by existing problems.

*There is implication to motivate change for 21ˢᵗ century FBO leadership performance to improve with new resources giving an option to examine and implement probable transformation using new constructs.*

²⁰ *Yes, each of you should remain, as you were when God called you.* ²¹ *Are you a slave? Do not let that worry you—but if you get a chance to be free, take it.* ²²*And remember, if you were a slave when the Lord called you, you are now free in the Lord. And, if you were free when the Lord called you, you are now a slave of Christ. (1Corinthians 7:20-22, NLT) Bible Gateway.*

# Purpose

The 1Corinthians verses above cite God calls disciples to serve with purpose requiring faithfulness and commitment. There is a specific entitlement for servants of God and teaching will help disciples to have comprehension of their identity in Christ. The recent research study by this author gave focus to determine whether leaders of FBOs struggle with unethical behavior hindering their purpose. There was determination, FBO leaders were not struggling with unethical behavior but requiring servant leaders and not leaders for FBOs. The experiential years of my spiritual journey introduces new leadership constructs for transforming and developing effective leaders. Leadership represents the embodiment of FBOs foundational performance to embrace community, culture, spirituality, and require authenticity.

Through the lens of the author, there is a view to perfect servant leader and not leader observing over twenty years subordinate leaders and senior clergy are probably leaders serving without a "calling". Leaders receiving the command "calling" by God might represent servant leaders that would undergird the faith-based organizational ecclesiastical experience converting individuals from worldly to spiritual commitment. The question posed for the study was whether ministering leaders of FBOs are characterizing servant leaders and were approachable to benefit a survey for evaluation.

Table 1

*Manual Score of Leadership Practices from LPIS*

| Name of FBO | DTW | ISV | CTP | SOA | PTH | | |
|---|---|---|---|---|---|---|---|
| Bethel AME | 709 | 693 | 700 | 717 | 712 | 3531 | 14 |
| Bethel Temple | 1145 | 1078 | 1119 | 1219 | 1160 | 5721 | 26 |
| Ivy Baptist Church | 1692 | 1586 | 1630 | 1783 | 1751 | 8442 | 35 |
| St. Paul Lutheran | 597 | 549 | 582 | 632 | 626 | 2986 | 13 |
| Smithfield Baptist | 452 | 400 | 417 | 528 | 504 | 2301 | 12 |
| Totals | 4595 | 4306 | 4448 | 4879 | 4753 | | $N=100$ |

The leadership evaluation provides a manual hand scoring with results indicating weaknesses and strengths. The survey was five denominations having five ethnicities within a local community consisting of $N=100$ cooperative respondents. The results are employable to support servant leader traits as leaders may be affecting followers needing transformation. False empowerment may exist in FBOs that exemplify corporate structure with an ecclesiastical façade for the 21st Century. Notably the results suggest Develop the Way (DTW) for the five FBOs of 4595 was lower than Sanction Others to Act (SOA) of 4879 and Persuade the Heart (PTH) 4753, but higher than 4306 Inspire and Share the Vision (ISV) and Confront the Process (CTP) 4448. Obeying God to resume studies for knowledge of Kouzes and Posner study of leadership behaviors it became perceptive that disciples are not benefiting teaching to image and exemplify Christ's character traits. However, Greenleaf's character traits of listening, awareness, community building, commitment growth, conceptualize, empathy, healing, foresight, persuasiveness, and steward can integrate with the behaviors by Kouzes and Posner as new leadership constructs.

Comprehending leadership type is important to authentically teach and train disciples to image Christ.

*4 Now the Holy Spirit tells us clearly that in the last times some will turn away from the true faith; they will follow deceptive spirits and teachings that come from demons. ² These people are hypocrites and liars, and their consciences are dead.[a] 1 Timothy 4:1-3NLT (Bible Gateway)*

# Types of Leaders

Paul is writing to Timothy in 1 Timothy 4:1-3 to instruct his leaders the Holy Spirit will clearly give guidance to avoid deception, demonic teachings and to stay true to their faith. Leaders require continuous teaching as deceptive voices they encounter daily can weaken the faith of individuals. Probably refuting discipleship teaching and Sunday school disqualifying Christian education is cause of false teachers having clergy assignments. The command by God to "called and uncalled" leaders to obey in Matthew 28:19-20 the Great Commission is to teach and train all nations to benefit true knowledge, growth, and relationship. Additionally, Matthew 28:19-20 infers Christ knew there were true and false leaders when after His resurrection he gave the command to the disciples. After resurrection, Christ was aware some disciples were believers and some were non-believers knowing the importance of teaching for disciples to serve the baptized believers letting them know he would always be present.

## Called/Uncalled Leaders

*This is what the LORD says—your Redeemer, the Holy One of Israel: "I am the LORD your God, who teaches you what is good for you and leads you along the paths you should follow. Isaiah 48:17 NLT (Bible Gateway)*

There is a spiritual anointing upon the "called' that the "uncalled" does not receive as it is an aura of God's spiritual

1

presence when he chooses His servant leaders with an assignment. Isaiah is hearing God say He teaches, leads him to obey, and follow reminding Isaiah He is, "His Redeemer" as God redeems us from our sinful deeds, desiring to use us as servant leaders. Servant leaders will serve with specific directions from God as they listen with awareness, conceptualizing how to carry out His assignment obediently. The word tells us God is present with all humankind, the just and the unjust having "uncalled" leaders that are individuals of self-gratification and accolades. A pretentious leader God is unable to communicate directives desiring leaders to be humble like Christ. Presently, senior clergy lack spiritual discernment choosing leaders not within God's plan for His people. The current-status of faith-based organizations exhibits "uncalled" leaders and not "called" servants as the "uncalled" select as employment option for "pastorship" having credible credentials.

The spiritual journey of this writer recollects FBO leaders were "called" with the gift of spiritual discernment to pastor imaging the characteristics of Christ the servant leader. The "called" leader using spiritual discernment knows who would become diaconates to assist with the body of believers employing Christian educational teaching for preparation. There is former experiential knowledge that a disciple in receiving God's command to a "call", inform the pastor, the pastor would send the disciple for training to comply obediently with the assignment. There are constituents becoming members in FBOs under senior pastors lacking spiritual discernment, unable to process new members giving directives for discipleship growth.

Through my experiential journey, it became knowledgeable there were external organizations available to assist local FBOs to structure the congregants for spiritual growth through teaching. Today, the external resource affiliations to assist FBO leaders, senior clergy are rejecting the tools that could communicate and build relationship to improve ministry.

*[13]Then he added, "Now go and learn the meaning of this Scripture: 'I want you to show mercy, not offer sacrifices.'[a] For I have come to call not those who think they are righteous, but those who know they are sinners."Matthew 9:13 NLT, (Bible Gateway).*

Matthew 9:13, some disciples assume they are righteous, unaware that Christ calls and cleanse sinners, not those who believe to be perfect that are unable to be a witnessing servant. A righteous disciple will find it impossible to witness to others indicating they have no scars or did any sinful actions. A witness that Christ cleanses and Calls would be a person that was set free from incarceration, a young girl pregnant out of wedlock, survivor from close to death illness to name a few. A disciple witnesses to others the experience knowing God give freedom from sinful actions and life cleansing to the unrighteous.

There is "uncalled" FBO leaders lack knowledge due to discontinuance of Christian education unaware continuous education enhances quality and qualifications to teach. Thereby, "uncalled" leaders are seeking employment at the (corporate America) salary scale that is non-relative to God's command for "called" servant leaders. "Uncalled" leaders desire to receive a salary at the corporate level and not amenable to the affordable salary of FBO. An "uncalled" leader accepting a servant assignment lacking passion should relinquish the position to have a "called" servant to represent Christ and his passion.

The "called" leaders responding to God's command to accept pastorship assignments could satisfy FBOs with qualifying credentials. Several "called" servant leaders have careers that might hinder the proficiency of pastorship receiving substantial earning not compelling the FBO to comply with monetary demands. On the other hand, if "called" leader retire from employment it is probable to accept FBOs affordable income with commitment to ecclesiastical service.

On this spiritual journey since seminarian studies and completing the Servant Leadership manuscript, it became spiritually commanding to do this writing for senior clergy to know there are specific behaviors for priestly duties. Seemingly, a minute percentage of "called" as opposed to large percentage of "uncalled" clergy are obtaining salary of corporate America CEO employment with full benefits choosing FBO pastorship. With Christian education an important foundation for FBOs, the "uncalled" and "called" leaders have unethical and immoral behaviors with attitudes affecting followers. Universally, education is a continuous paradigm for Continuing Education in universities.

***II Timothy 4:15, study to show thyself approved, a workman need not to be ashamed, rightly dividing the word of God.***

The verse affirms Paul want "called" leaders/teachers to recognize that God requires consistency of study for effective leadership gives knowledge and unequivocal truth of Gods' Word. Christian education should be the underpinning for the body of believers as researchers reference leaders in FBO are unspiritual and unchristian developing barriers disqualifying continuous education. II Timothy 4:15, Paul informing Timothy could be an applicable message for the new millennium leaders to receive and obediently respond for continuous knowledge and spiritual growth. Tele-ministry is modes through radio, television and internet that is convenient to access for knowledge unaware of its authenticity of leaders representation.

Greenleaf, 2008 study addressing the construct of servant leadership became an essential component for improving the role of the "called" leaders for FBOs in the 21st century. Additionally, his original study of 1977 was an enlightenment of servant leadership theory of young people at that time revolting against behaviors of university staff workers. It was noteworthy Greenleaf's profundity for the young peoples' revolt gave principles for leadership character traits. The 1977 research for profit and nonprofit organizations represents leaders universally serving the public, subordinates and scholars. Further editing of his study in 2009 gave identification to institutions as businesses, governments, armies, churches, and universities with all organizations holding people responsible.

Servant leadership is a phrase coined by Robert Greenleaf in his work *The Servant as Leader,* published in 1970 and revised in 2008. Researchers are still expanding upon Greenleaf's concept informing people of the benefit to act as a servant, not a leader.

Exploring the history of servant leadership gave extensive support to the concept that servant leadership is genuine leadership while defining servant leader attributes. It was possible to investigate leadership through articles, journals, and research documents for theories of general leadership, spiritual leader and servant leadership. Several experts in Christian doctrine have implied that faith-based leaders need to be servant leaders. Researching theorists for leader's behaviors and attitudes that might affect followers in the FBOs, Kouzes and Posner with Robert Greenleaf resource is the essential content to transform profit and nonprofit FBOs. Historically, proponents of servant leadership have used the Bible to support the concept of servant leaders as in

*[43] But among you, it will be different. Whoever wants to be a leader among you must be your servant, [44] and whoever wants to be first among you must be the slave of everyone else. (Mark 10:43-44, NLT, Bible Gateway)*

The servant leader resource gives characteristic traits for disciples to comprehend there is a lifestyle for faith believers of Christ. Leaders require knowledge they are servant leaders that through Christian education they could have classes to teach and train presenting the opportunity to minister. Until individuals have clarity of leader and servant leader, leaders will characterize traits believing leadership is an "I" syndrome-losing sight of representing a "slave" to serve as Christ.

[21] If you keep yourself pure, you will be a special utensil for honorable use. Your life will be clean, and you will be ready for the Master to use you for every good work. *2 Timothy 2:21, NLT (Bible Gateway)*

The word further addresses the servant leader and its lifestyle implicating it is to be pure and clean to be ready for the exceptional assignment that God desires for His disciples. Disciples are to be ready, willing to accept the assignment requiring no specific gender, age, color, or ethnicity, just to respond with "yes Lord" requiring preparation. Therefore, perpetual teaching and training is necessary for the FBO to make available with a Christian educator programming the studies.

Teach me how to live, O Lord. Lead me along the right path, for my enemies are waiting for me.
Psalm 27:11 NLT (Bible Gateway).

Christian educators are imperative for FBOs to teach disciples how to live and receive instructions to avoid satanic forces to give response to their calling. If disciples are serving as Christ spoke in Matthews 28:20 to disciple others by teaching, then hearing David affirm to teach the word would not be difficult for servants to please God.

Some leaders do not comprehend servitude as an essential component of leadership with Greenleaf revising his 1972 publication *The Institution as Servant,* supportive with scripture, to be a leader individuals are to become a servant. Of further reference, Greenleaf chose the three institutional types based on his personal experiences as clergy, professor and manager. Recognizing Greenleaf's various roles of employment became his belief to use his new model for servant leadership for at least one of the institutions to improve performance of communication, and quality within the organization.

The several researchers referencing leadership constructs did require comparisons of theories to understand implications and purpose of achieving effective changes. Comparison defines types of leaders, interactions of leaders with followers and situations. Although Greenleaf, Kouzes and Posner's traits and standards introduces behaviors with standards but not types of leaders, comparison of general, spiritual and servant leadership is to merit transformation of performance.

## General Leadership

General leadership is a title of intense study throughout the 21st century with several theorists implicating concepts to influence followers without specific title of spiritual or servant leaders. A researcher expressed a phenomenal remark about leaders and leadership stating leaders are comparable to an artist with their intuitiveness and creativity in performance of their work. This reference became pervasive to teaching spiritual gifting informing the scholars, "You are a unique masterpiece" with a gifting purpose. The uniqueness of each believer being a masterpiece of art soon develops an identity, builds self-esteem feeling strength and capability to serve God. There is recollection of a Sunday school lesson on "Creation" at the early age of thirteen experiencing low self-esteem, sadden about life, learning that God's love uniquely designed me, gave new beginnings to life overcoming the past. This gives rise to why Christian education is vital for thousands ages 0 to 100 broken within, requiring resolution of their pain and past hurts for healing and renewal.

[2] After dark one evening, he came to speak with Jesus. "Rabbi," he said, "we all know that God has sent you to teach us. Your miraculous signs are evidence that God is with you." John 3:2 NLT (Bible Gateway)

Jesus is teaching Nicodemus a Pharisee and religious leader, recognizing Christ as a "Rabbi" in Hebrew is Master Teacher with respect to his miraculous proof to teach with knowledge and power from God. Each disciple (servant) is to know they are recipients of the Holy Spirit from God with Matthew 28:20 affirming that God's presence is always with his servant leaders in all that they will do to please Him.

The 21st century is identifying leaders and leadership qualities that are rising and falling without defining any determining qualities once they benefit knowledge of their gifting. Research data inform that leadership is an elusive construct to develop literature for organizational behavior especially true with media circulating unethical and immoral issues of leaders at ecclesiastic and corporate America status. There is truth that leaders are taking risks, as their role is essential for organizational followership making decisions and satisfying the commitment for growth of people and organization. Leaders are to recognize the task-at-hand of servant leader that influences relationship with intent to grow an organization and transform for the good of society a multidirectional performance between their role and followers.

## Servant Leadership

[2] *"Look, I have specifically chosen Bezalel son of Uri, grandson of Hur, of the tribe of Judah. Exodus 31:2, NLT (Bible Gateway)*

God will choose a servant that cannot reject but be receptive to discipleship with honor and respect to the assignment by serving diligently and obediently as new leader. God gave assistance to the new leader, Bezalel by choosing others that would support the leadership assignment with specific instructions to obey. Should FBO have Christian educational structure in the FBO for disciples to learn their purpose in Christ, they would be as Bezalel and not face concealment as Nicodemus to benefit knowledge for servant leader.

Servant leadership is a phrase coined by Robert Greenleaf in his work *The Servant Leader,* published in 1970 and revised in 2008. Researchers since 1970 have been broadening Greenleaf's concept informing people about servant and not leader character traits.

Servant leader is not a new entitlement for leaders of FBOs as Christ is the ultimate servant leader for disciples to exemplify as believing followers. The essence of servant leader is they serve selflessly and selfishly, as there are leaders lacking understanding of being a servant first and a leader second. Additional viewpoint to recognize is that Greenleaf' study views servant leader following a calling to serve others responding to ethics and abiding laws of God. The fact that two other researchers were acknowledging additional paradigms gives affirmation for transformation at the 21$^{st}$ century for FBOs.

Research indicates in recent years there have been attention to servant leaders and implementing standards within organizations. The indication refers to media and press releases trying to assess leadership and its authenticity. In addition, the thought to consider is leadership authenticity comparable to God's authenticity of "calling" and not individuals selecting leaders. Authenticity could be visible when disciples receiving teaching and training will demonstrate image of Christ to other disciples and sharing the word to enhance their growth. Growth begins with disciple receiving "milk" 1 Peter 2:2 and as they continue to grow gradually goes from milk to meat of the word Hebrew 5:12-14. The growth and development through the word has its similarities to infant birth to maturity of adulthood in how much disciples are able to learn and understand from the Word of God receiving its truths. It is through this teaching developmental experience the Christians (disciples) maturity level of faith grows. There is the opportunity of disciples taking an assessment of their spiritual growth that determines the level of maturity that will be available in the accompanying study guide.

Research recommends there is the need to assess for leadership authenticity constructs that might be a unique contribution for positive results to transform leaders to servant leaders. There is contention through research study of servant leadership that leaders with visions can implement the visions and define direction for an organization. The servant leader concept is essential, as they are servants first desiring to help people become successful, responding to needs and interests of others with aspiration. Greenleaf's introduction of servant leader concept is a derivative of the foundational teaching of Jesus Christ and biblical accounts and not an original idea.

Could it be possible the leadership format for a football coach be comparable to a servant leader serving FBO give effective leadership performance? Another scenario, a Disney World crowd concept of people attracting constituents to church, and would this action be theological? It is possible for principles applicable for football coaches and Disney officials to be employable .for influencing effective leadership performance in faith-based organizations. The two formats are employable for increasing constituents, as they are applicable to gather people and not to teach theology.

After Greenleaf 1972 study was creative with the term in his first essay as "Servant as Leader", there was the establishment of the Greenleaf Leadership Center in Westfield, Indiana that continues to produce revision editions of Greenleaf's work for additional concepts for servant leadership. Faith followers (called) today are facing challenges of ineffective leadership lacking comprehension of the character of Christ requiring continuous teaching that is the foundation for FBOs.

When a leader acknowledges the authenticity of their role, it makes a difference in performance and avoids global indifferences in society for FBOs. The goal of the resource is to define, and compare leaders with servant leader using the research data of character traits to provide in-depth insight to improve abilities and effectiveness of leaders in FBOs. Servant leaders have identifying qualities of the heart, head, hands and habits to model within FBOs, serving the people as humble stewards being mindful of what they say and do as they care for the followers. Long before the existence of other researchers' study developing leadership character traits, Christ was the ultimate servant leader that gives an image for leaders universally.

For example, the following behavioral traits are for successful leadership as a servant:

- *Commitment:* Leader's affects others with their behavior of commitment that determines if others will follow them.
- *Obedience:* When a leader demonstrates obedience, it is a leader serving from the heart imaging for others a great motivator.
- *Humility and selflessness:* Leaders displaying humility and selflessness are experiencing positive consequential action with followers trust him as the leader thinks less of self and places others first.
- *Sacrifice:* A true leader will demonstrate an interest from the heart for others through serving ignoring *self.*
- *Passion:* A passionate servant leader will suffer and consider others as Christ.
- *Energetic:* A leader serving others for a cause demonstrating zeal, excitement and enthusiasm is an energetic servant for God.
- *Relational:* A Servant leader with the ability to engage others, belief in others as this is important. When leaders develop and maintain personal and organizational vitality, there is a relationship between followers and leaders.

*Dr. Shirley A. Young*

*As an obedient servant, I gave response to God's request to pursue a research study for servant leadership benefitting knowledge that the image of Christ is lost requiring restoration. It affirms the gratification of obedience to an assignment that was unclear believing irrelevant to becoming relevant for profit and nonprofit organizations. The relevancy introduces R. Greenleaf (2008) ten character traits to transform organizational leadership universally.*

# Discuss Disciples and Teaching

Disciples are individuals consenting to accept a spiritual life style within a denomination of faith adhering to a doctrine of faith with anticipation to receive teaching and training for spiritual growth to maintain the commitment of their faith.

There are various Christian faith groups teaching biblical concepts to enhance the spiritual life of disciples to learn their gifting for ministering to others. Specifically, the Methodist and Presbyterian denominations mandate teaching their laity/lay-members to grow in knowledge and purpose of servant leadership to develop others in the kingdom of God.

The importance of teaching is to receive biblical knowledge for spiritual growth that resembles parents developing their child to grow from infancy to maturity to be an asset for society. Individuals develop relationship with God and one another enrich their spiritual experience.

The FBOs did receive the great commission of Matthew 28:20 go to all nations and make disciples to change minds, hearts and behaviors teaching to become servant leaders influencing Christ to others for Kingdom building. This knowledge appears beyond comprehension for current senior clergy as corporate representatives of large FBOs ranging in thousands (3,000 to about 10,000) as all senior clergy are not "called".

For disciples to benefit maturity they require continuous teaching that seemingly the "Baptist" faith considers obsolete and unimportant to implement. Christian education is not a financial expense as Christian educators volunteer, not salaried, assuming the failure to sanction the Great Commission derive from "uncalled" leaders without the anointing of God's spiritual move upon their heart and mind. Clergy "called" or "uncalled" should address the importance of what to do with disciples, or become aware of having disciples/members, or recognize disciples according to a number and not disregard the importance of a disciple.

Disciples represent sheep, clergy represents shepherd, and the word of God requires shepherds to feed the sheep for growth that is through teaching and training by Christian educators. Serving as servant leader through the experiential journey, FBOs employ spiritual gift assessment for new disciple orientation classes that evaluate new servants to know their gifting. FBOs benefit receiving a Christian educator as some are by recommendation or "calling". There is an important question, "Can secular teachers teach in the Christian educational ministry"? Secular teachers are acceptable if they are amenable to the FBOs protocol to teach and have training within the organizations.

When an FBO establish sessions for disciples to benefit knowledge for ministering at the conclusion of teaching sessions can a secular teacher satisfy qualification to perform? An FBO with polity and doctrinal rules determine if individuals will minister upon completion of the studies. It is definitely essential to have Christian educational teaching with training for the influx of members within FBOs of all denominations having knowledge that this is plummeting and extraneous. Discipleship teaching should be the foundation for FBOs to fulfill God's desire for a relationship with His people through his son Jesus Christ, who lived, bled and died to free humankind from sin for the gift of salvation.

# Leadership Character Traits

Theocentric trait emulation of Christ the ultimate servant leader of faith-based organizations (FBOs) will be inclusive in the study. Research supports Greenleaf's 2008, 2009 origin of servant leader concept referencing Christ being relative to biblical data as ultimate servant leader. The following list of character traits images Christ and with Christian educational teaching and training, each disciple could transform with new constructs to influence other followers.

## Humility

[12] *Since God chose you to be the holy people he loves, you must clothe yourselves with tenderhearted mercy, kindness, humility, gentleness, and patience. Colossians 3:12NLT (Bible Gateway*

A humble servant leader emulates Christ the ultimate servant leader who prior to committing his life to the Roman soldiers, had communion with the twelve disciples washing of their feet, excepting one disciple, Judas saying he was unworthy. Colossians Church 3:12 informs the servants God chose them to clothe in character of humility and mercy as holy people he will love. A humble servant demonstrating gentleness, patience and kindness would grow with the image of Christ influencing other disciples.

## Awareness/Perception

*The trait of awareness is recognizable with the disciples engaging Christ's attention of an adulterous woman to receive punishment for her sinful life. Christ perception of the disciples' behavior became silent, stooping to appear to ignore their question, imparted a question of whether anyone was perfect without sin. The question exhibits Christ perceiving the disciples could not answer and aware they would disappear recognizing they were guilty as the woman. (John 3-11, NLT Bible Gateway).*

A leader can frame their awareness with accompanying sensory and perceptional experiences. Individuals can have a narrow perception with a minute experience to cause missing the grandeur. In John 3:11, the disciples were missing the essence of Christ's awareness about the adulterous woman, as Christ did not look at her former action but what was in her favor. It speaks to one of us today, our behavior is immoral and it is after facing consequences, there is reconciliation available to give justification. When this awareness is recognizable, it gives a person favor to overcome their disparity, as with the adulterous woman and Christ being aware of her issue. The overall defining of awareness/perception involves trust, incorporating values with motives, cognition and feelings. Servant leaders would exhibit unique capabilities, knowledge, from experiences that equip them to lead with essential mechanism for achieving clarity in leadership vision.

There is recommendation to review perception as an opportunity to test tolerance levels using awareness traits. Leaders having an awareness experience vary with obligations and responsibilities by sorting urgent from important issues and process issues in an effective order. The trait of awareness is uncomfortable, disturbing feelings and yet enlightening moments, with stressful experiences that can find composure permitting an opportunity to manage.

Observing servant leaders today in a local FBO, awareness/ perception traits are lacking, as it is unknown to 21ˢᵗ century disciples, particularly, where to find teaching. The discovery during the research study was that not all researchers considered awareness/perception as a trait for the servant leader. Of the several researchers considering character traits, there is recognition by Greenleaf using a theological concept, as others did not select for consideration in their study.

## Empathy

*The text of two blind men sitting by the side of the road as Jesus was on his Jericho journey is an example of a servant leader responding with empathy to the needs of others. In this setting, "Jesus felt sorry for them" implicating his empathy. (Matt 20:29-34, Bible Gateway)*

Greenleaf's 2008 study indicates the character trait of empathy is feelings for another as in Matthew 20 exhibiting the character of a servant leader with empathy while on the Jericho Road Journey. Christ was conscious of setting an example for all disciples witnessing the healing having confidence in their empathetic leader. Christ the ultimate servant leader demonstrates good leadership using his emotions with respect of the disciples observing his approach, displaying his compassion and concern, allowing an influence of judgment to activate. When servant leaders exhibit trust with empathy as a foundational element of acceptance it will have followers influence trusting.

## Healing

To identify "healing" as a leader trait, Greenleaf while doing his 1977 study did conduct it in a seminary of varying faiths knowing that Christ demonstrates the purest form of servant leadership.

> *One example involved the healing of the Samaritan. "He fell to the ground at Jesus' feet, thanking Him for what He had done. This man was a Samaritan" (Luke 17:16 NLT, Bible Gateway).*

Christ, the ultimate servant leader, performed healings that influenced many people. When Christ healed 10 lepers with only 1 returning to thank Him. Later, the leper became a Samaritan who gave glory and honor to God for healing his leprosy. (Luke 17:11-19 NLT, Bible Gateway). The leper story is an example of how spirituality in leadership can involve an action of influence to cause people to serve others. Christ came to heal and deliver humankind desiring to have a relationship developing into a disciple. Disciples growing spiritually, will evidence healing as a witness, influencing others to God through Christ.

Disciples grow spiritually through witnessing Christ is evidence of healing and they serve others influencing Christ.

## Foresight

> *Christ did experience rejection having wisdom, young, a carpenter's son, spoke with intellect and astonishment to his community recognizing he would depart into far distance to those who are believers (Matthew 13:53-58, NLT).*

Observation of the FBOs foresight is a pertinent character trait for current leaders for projecting the future. Taking a glimpse of the definition of foresight during the research study in relinquishing Christian education is probable cause of ethical failure in leadership. When servant leaders use foresight, they will lead effectively as opposed to leaders not using foresight-having fear of losing their leadership position by not improving the process becomes a serious ethical compromise.

## Persuasion

An effective servant leader is persuasive having personal source of power to include knowledge, effort and expertise. A leader using the persuasive character trait will persuade a direct appeal to the organizational followers to achieve a direct outcome, exhibiting persuasion to convince others and not demonstrate coercion.

*Galatians 5:7-9 Paul speaks to the Galatians church of their faltering after showing good faith and progress, asking why they suddenly stopped to listen to false leaders causing non- influence to others.*

There are advantages to the character trait of persuasiveness that are obvious as leaders can use persuasion as a gentle method to initiate change. Additionally, leaders will use the power of persuasion with disadvantages by coercing others with power to dominate and manipulate people (their followers). Paul with the Galatians church became concerned, as they were doing great, making giant steps in the race, and then suddenly waning as the FBO today is regressing with no Christian educational teaching for spiritual growth.

Today FBOs are persuasively evidencing power to create alternative opportunities to allow leaders to choose and build their autonomy. Observation of persuasive empowerment is coercively clairvoyant in FBO leadership ministry. The character of persuasion is an effective and positive trait for servant leaders as it sanction the leader to offer hope to the hopeless and allow followers to view they are empowered in lieu of leaders being empowered.

Alternatively, coercion endures as long as there is an existing force supporting coercion that is not organic; persuasion is organic involving voluntary acceptance of influence being selfishly used is manipulative with political scheming.

An appeal to FBO leaders to reconsider the resumption of Christian education to give disciples teaching and training that benefit knowledge of being a servant leader with character traits imaging Christ. Additionally, the disciple will benefit knowledge of their identity in Christ and spiritual gifting for purpose of serving Christ. It is astonishing to realize that leaders across the states have discontinued Christian education ignoring the Word of God.

II Timothy 2: 15 *we must work hard so that as disciples we can present self to God to receive his approval. Be a good worker, one who does not need to be ashamed and who correctly explains the word of truth.*

## Stewardship

Stewardship is a performance that is weighty and influential for managing leaders as trustees protect values and is the culture of an organization being instrumental in creating high organization performance. Additionally, the leader possesses ultimate trust to administer the institute or organization with careful responsibility.

*Jesus tells his disciples the parable of a shrewd manager working for a rich man found to be dishonest facing termination of his job. The manager did not want to face his consequences and thought to involve the other workers to have them pay back their debts by reducing it making it possible to repay giving him saving grace of his job. (Luke 16:1-10, NLT, Bible Gateway).*

The text gives a primary concern for the steward's responsibility and the assets of the rich man' resources, how the manager (steward) went about managing the problem. It is the task of a steward to resolve issues within the organization, as it was imperative for the manager to do in the text especially needing to survive maintaining his job. There will be conflict arising in organizations, the leader having character traits, as a steward is able to resolve the issues such as this *shrewd manager* was able to accomplish. When servant leader's exercises character traits of stewardship they are developing internal leadership structures with administrative culture for the organization. There is a major responsibility of using critical thinking to resolve the issues within the organization such as the *shrewd manager* became cognitive of needing his job. Using the biblical analogy gives recognition to workers today that take pens, pencils, paper clips, paper, etc is pilfering supplies from organizations, an invisible infraction against the monthly expenses.

The following features steward should possess, legitimacy that begins with trust, if there is lack of trust, there will be decrease in productivity as this can cause major decline in large institutions. Leaders of FBOs are experiencing blind trust that includes respect for authority and trust generating leadership charisma proposing that trust begins with stewardship character traits of leaders accepting the responsibility to design a new culture. Additionally notable, leaders with stewardship characteristics are in demand to oversee administrators and assist them in moving an organization toward excellence. To further mention, trustees should be exploitive with their inside-outside objective position to be an instrument of understanding.

## Listening

Servant leaders are to exemplify Christ having the listening trait that provides insight as Christ a true listener responding to resolve many issues having no respect of person. Servant leaders having the character of listening first, being true and natural would provide automatic response to a problem.

Further, listening intently gives comprehension and ability to process assignments more effectively and the importance to hear as a true listener gives the desire to communicate. A servant leader will have no problem listening, to build up others with trust that is crucial reflecting the ability to listen as effective listening needs another person total attention looking directly at him or her. A leader with effective listening permits followers to benefit understanding, resist becoming defensive, being cognitive of defensive feelings from followers.

*James says you must all be quick to listen, slow to speak, and slow to get angry (James 1:19, NLT, Bible Gateway).*

The text supports the servant leaders' character of listening with silence avoiding anger paying attention to defensive behavior.

## Conceptualization

Not many researchers gave consideration of conceptualization as a character trai**t with Greenleaf an i**mportant choice discovering his study gives a leaders' trait that could process conceptualization illustrating their experiences to guide current organizations.

Conceptualization could be relative to foresight (another trait) basing it on a leader's ability to foresee the probable future. Servant leaders are to expand their minds to embrace expansive conceptual thinking with their "calling" that will give subtle balance between conceptual thoughts to focus approaches. Leaders conceptualizing would require discipline and practice as it is a characteristic for servant leaders to expand their thinking that would encompass broad based conceptual thinking.

Greenleaf's study did raise a question how should people develop the ability to act and improve the quality of thinking that recognizes people with the ability to comprehend increasing complex and interrelational realities. When a servant leader understands the deep forces that would shape reality, instead of just correcting a problem, this is conceptual leadership.

## Community Building

Community building is not an actual trait but an active accomplishment that servant leaders will perform with recommendation that leaders celebrate values and victories to create a spirit of community. The leaders' character develops in a community through displaying humility to perform with submission to rebuild a viable community requiring adequate attendance of people.

## Commitment

Servant leaders should have the character trait of commitment as it represents loyalty toward strengthening an organization, exhibiting positive attitudes toward the organization. Additionally, if leaders use their heart and mind, commitment will involve maintaining motivation and internal belief. Further indications, a leader's commitment will affect the follower's determination as servant leader's commitment influences followers. It is critical to observe competency and character during communication of essential issues as this develops the leader's commitment over time. Leaders with competence and confidence develop commitment that gives empowerment. The empowerment supports a leader's ability to identify challenges, analyze strengths of commitment, and encourage risk taking.

## Leader Initiative

Leader initiative takes the risk of failure while aiming for success being innovative, implementing new ideas and structure. The character trait is what a leader should possess to seize the opportunity using positive attitudes and actions for excellent results. Servant leaders initiate engaging their staff to set high standards, excel in performance, and communicate their belief of success. Servant leaders exemplify with innovation, stay sensitive to external realities, embrace improvement, and inspire others, as the motivation will originate from their "calling" and not just a job.

## Leader Integrity

A servant leader's integrity should represent the inner values that are of consistency with outward words and actions, as their integrity will help followers to expect consistency from the leader. A leaders' consistency of speech and perspective develops trust with confidence to their followers for planning as opposed to being unpredictable losing integrity of trust, as trust is the foundation of integrity. Furthermore, there is indication a servant leader should exhibit reliability and honesty that would create trust in followers, as followers may not agree with the ideas or desire to support the actions.

FBO servant leaders with a "calling" should image integrity with consistency of commitment to gain respect of others that would avoid possible conflicts as leaders receive continuous support preventing decline in their integrity. It is arduous to continuously support and trust a servant leader after losing their integrity as they represent accountability, creativity with efficiency for pursuing excellence in service.

*An example to consider is when God questioned Satan asking if he was considering testing Job a man of complete integrity that fears the Lord (Job 2:3 Bible Gateway).*

*Another example is David pleads for his innocence knowing he was performing with integrity, keeping his trust in God and unwavering (Psalm 26:1 Bible Gateway).*

FBOs are not intentional with educating and training leaders that permit assessing all leaders that will determine the weaknesses and strengths of character traits that should exemplify Christ.

# FIVE LEADERSHIP STANDARDS

# Develop the Way Theory

Kouzes and Posner's research study for profit and nonprofit organizations supports all levels of institutions recognizing this resource improves leaders/followers for transformation. The five standards require servant leaders to commit to: (1) developing the way, (2) inspire and share a vision, (3) confront the process, (4) sanction others to act, and (5) persuade the heart for leaders to perform with Christ-like behaviors (See Table 2).

Further, commitment is identifiable as a servant leader's character trait during research of Kouzes and Posner's study with comparison to R. Greenleaf' study. There is a specific implication since reviewing the five standards denoting commitment in each performance that correlates with traits of listening and stewardship.

The first leadership standard develop the way associates with opportunity to (a) clarify self and find your voice to affirm sharing ideals, (b) how to set examples for others to share their values. The character trait of commitment can grow individuals and followers' as it is important to build up community. Leaders demonstrating commitment to build communities have two inclusive traits for developing their way (See table 3).

The second leadership standard is to inspire and share a vision. Using this standard, leaders are able to (a) imagine possibilities by envisioning the future and can (b) appeal and enlist others to share their vision with their aspirations. Leaders employing the character traits of awareness, foresight, and listening can correlate exercising commitment that will grow other leaders. Conceptualizing another trait engages leaders to share excitement visualizing the future to enable possibilities and maintain commitment.

The third leadership standard will confront the process for leaders to challenge and exhibit stewardship another trait and (a) obtain innovative ways to take risks, experiment, improve to generate successes and (b) learn from the experiences. The character trait of persuasion could correlate to the concept of *confronting the process* as a leaders' concept often uses persuasion to attain support from others when taking risks. It is a recommendation for leaders to evaluate their strengths and weaknesses when considering changes within groups of the organization.

The fourth leadership standard is to sanction others to act performing two elements requiring leadership commitment (a) build trust and facilitate relationships with others (b) enhance developing self-determination and competence in others. Additionally, there are two other character traits specifically *empathy* and *conceptualization* that correlates to the commitment elements. When a leader exercises *empathy*, a leader becomes sensitive while building trust with others. Leaders demonstrating the traits of *conceptualization, awareness, and healing* promote cooperative goals using their discretion. Of further note, a leader's personality with perception and conceptualization would be consistent with their characteristic behavior.

Finally, the fifth standard is to persuade the heart with two elements of (a) exhibiting appreciation, with recognition of individual excellence, and (b) celebrating victories and values creating a spirit of community. There were other theorists reflecting traits of healing, empathy, and building community that does give leaders the opportunity to enhance their commitment as a steward.

Table 2 is a diagram of the traits and standards for reference indicating commitment and for developing the standards while enhancing the traits of behaviors.

Table 2

*Five Standards and Ten Commitments of Leadership*

| Practice | Commitment |
|---|---|
| 1. Develop the way | a. Affirm your voice |
| | b. Set an example |
| 2. Inspire and share a vision | c. Visualize the future |
| | d. Recruit others |
| 3. Confront the process | e. Pursue opportunities |
| | f. Assess by risk taking |
| 4. Sanction others to act | g. Promote collaboration |
| | h. Reinforce others |
| 5. Persuade the heart | i. Distinguish contributions |
| | j. Commemorate the values and Victories |

Developing a way becomes a confrontation for leaders to strengthen their abilities that could make a positive difference in society (See Table 3). Developing a new model for individuals to pattern is a belief the theory would develop effective leaders introducing new skills and abilities practical to enhance and motivate followers. After tedious research, it was appreciative to benefit two authors collaborating to improve leadership in profit and nonprofit organizational performance introducing new constructs. Table 3 shows a comparison between their theories of standards and traits that might appear different but relative for leadership transformation.

The author's contention to do comparison could be employable to determine if the attributes are applicable for leaders, managers, subordinates, or servant leaders.

Table 3

*Comparison of Develop the Way to Ten Character Traits*

| Five Standards | Character Traits of Greenleaf |
| --- | --- |
| Develop the Way | Listening |
| Inspire and share a vision | Empathy |
| Confront the process | Healing |
| Sanction others to act | Awareness |
| Persuade the heart | Persuasion |
| | Conceptualization |
| | Foresight |
| | Stewardship |
| | Commitment for growth |
| | Community building |

The objective for the new constructs is for leaders to transform to servant leaders to inspire a shared vision, by confronting the process, to sanction others to perform persuading their hearts to follow new traits that would enhance performance to image Christ influencing followers.

There is recognition of R. Greenleaf being the first author to develop the term *"servant leader"* with scriptural support of Christ's character emulating the traits and behaviors, as Christ served others at risk to Himself and not for a reward. A servant leader is not dependent upon receiving rewards, is an ultimate example of a leader encouraging collaboration and strengthens individuals, having no formal organizational power, a servant leader influences others.

There is evidence when leaders influence others as to leaders refuting character traits that would image Christ affecting the ethics of leaders' performance within the organizations. Determining the spiritual aspect of leadership is important based on Greenleaf's use of Jesus Christ as the ultimate servant leader.

# Comparison of General Leadership to Spiritual Leadership

Leadership theories are comparable introducing paradigms for FBOs to transition from basic secular performance to effective ecclesiastic performance. The research discussion for general leadership was propositional with other theorists presenting leadership factors reflecting a difference with spiritual and secular. There was benefit to the research being able to introduce new leaders' constructs of behaviors and traits to the organizational leadership field.

There were several publications of *Spiritual Leadership* with revisions giving support to this resource implicating when a Christian perceive a calling from the spirit of God, they listen, follow directions, plan and perform with commitment. It cannot be emphasized enough of the importance of continuing education for servant leaders in every genre of organizations. This discussion gives clarity of spiritual leadership and servant leadership. Servant leaders serve with an influential image when comparing to spiritual leadership based on qualities (See Table 4). Contrasting qualities with style provides a relationship between the spiritual leader and the servant leader to be different.

There is recommendation that leaders should receive training to be servant leaders and/or spiritual leaders to develop role model emulating Christ for others to follow. After training takes effect, a leader begin to exercise commitment, exhibiting a level of competence recognizing a leadership type with character traits for serving to make changes for the FBO. It is important for servant leaders to have humility, listening, patience and integrity to emulate Christ naming just a few characteristic traits, either influencing or not influencing followers, but ultimately image Christ.

Table 4

*Character Traits for Spiritual Leaders*

| Positive Qualities | Perilous Qualities |
| --- | --- |
| Patience | Egotism |
| Wisdom | Pride |
| Humility | Infallibility |
| Vision | Popularity |
| Courage | Depression |
| Decision | Indispensability and Pride |
| Humor | Elation/depression |
| Holy Anger | Depression |
| Integrity | Prolong position holding |
| Discipline | Competiveness |
| Tact | Failure/Greed |
| Inspirational Power | Mental laziness |
| Listening | Spiritual Lethargy |
| Written Communications | Mental laziness |
| Friendship | Spiritual lethargy |
| Executive abilities | Secular |

*The approach of comparison from theory to fact for spiritual and servant leaders respond to God seeking servants and not leaders. A pertinent probability is that senior clergy are dumbing-down constituents for Christian intellect by not teaching disciples to grow into servant leaders. Comparing spiritual to servant leadership recognizes character traits influencing pitfalls for servant leader to affect leadership standards.*

# Comparison of Spiritual Leadership to Servant Leadership

The comparison of traits for spiritual and servant leadership are employable to identifying the essential characteristics to serve in FBOs. The theory that servant leaders have character traits is invaluable and can be applicable, effective for increasing FBOs.

Spiritual and servant leaders are both of consideration for secular and Christian organizations as God is not looking for leaders, but looking for servants. Isaiah 59:16, Ezekiel 22:30 affirm the fact that a leadership position is not an occupation but it is a calling from God as a survey was reflective of people working solely for an *income* and not out of their *calling*. Initially, the assumption for the research of leadership at the top level of FBOs was displaying immoral and unethical actions to followers. Leaders of various FBO genres, for-profit, nonprofit, education, and government agencies were inclusive for examination by other researchers. Research data became a benefit of knowledge through observation of leadership in the local active organization near the town of my residence. The resources during the research study implicate Christian leaders could apply standards to accomplish extraordinary things within their organizations.

There were excellent results from a researcher's leadership practice inventory discovering specific behaviors of leaders to develop an introduction to new constructs. Introduction of the new constructs refutes the belief only a few men and women are capable of leading followers to greatness. The new constructs of traits and standards comprise influences and fundamental pitfalls characterizing leaders that affect followers either in a positive or negative direction.

Sources of negative influences are position, power, and personality, while, positive sources of influence include integrity, courage, and evidence of successful accomplishments, humility, with preparation exhibiting God's hand upon leaders. Spiritual leaders have pitfalls causing failure in their leadership assignment that influences foolish decisions disqualifying their activeness. The hindrances that prevent developing the character of a spiritual leader is pride, mental laziness, greed, spiritual lethargy, oversensitivity, domestic neglect, administrative carelessness with prolonging time within a position.

Spiritual and servant leadership traits will influence followers to grow spiritually should they perform with effective leadership tasking. See Table 5 for influences and pitfalls that leaders can characterize identifying integrity and pride that leaders use to encourage the heart of others.

Table 5

A Table listing of influences and pitfalls

| Influences | Pitfalls |
|---|---|
| Preparation | Pride |
| Personality | Oversensitivity |
| Power | Spiritual lethargy |
| Successful record accomplishment | Greed |
| Humility | Mental laziness |
| God's hand | Administrative carelessness |
| Courage | Domestic neglect |
| Integrity | Prolonged position holding |
| Position | "I" Syndrome |

# Importance of Christian Education

According to biblical text Christ and Paul emphasize teaching through Christian Education is vital for clergy to maintain to grow disciples speaking through the following verses.

*Great Commission, go teach all nations. After resurrection, Christ gave the disciples instruction to go and make disciples to the far ends of the world. Matthew 28:20 (NLT) Bible Gateway.*

Disciples require teaching and training to benefit knowledge to teach other disciples that all will obey the Great Commission. This is a continuous assignment to never end as disciples expand to the far corners of the world reaching others, responding with obedience as servant leaders.

*In those days I will pour out my Spirit, even on my servants—men and women alike- and they will prophesy. Acts 2:18 (NLT) Bible Gateway*

Acts 2:18 is an encouraging word to servants of God promise to pour out the Holy Spirit on men and women servants to prophesy that will be one of the many gifts God gives to disciples. Servants will receive their gifting according to Acts as it moves through the Holy Spirit, not man's empowerment but through Christian education in the FBO.

*- The false teachers will turn the minds of the disciples from lack of teaching and it will make them ignorant of the Word. 1 Timothy 4:1-3 (NLT) Bible Gateway*

The FBO is unable to escape false teachers and is why Christian education is the foundational purpose to try to avert true disciples from the influence of false servants that could weaken their faith and worship experience.

- *²¹ If you keep yourself pure, you will be a special utensil for honorable use. Your life will be clean, and you will be ready for the Master to use you for every good work. 2 Timothy 2:21 (NLT) Bible Gateway*

Paul second letter to Timothy speak to disciples they are special and to remain unpolluted and a special vessel with preparation to serve. Disciples require Christian Education to have spotless lifestyle and remain ready for Christ to use for every assignment.

Timothy like many other servant leaders for God has the responsibility after receiving disciples to grow disciples.

- *¹⁵ Be careful of him, for he fought against everything we said. ¹⁶ The first time I was brought before the judge, no one came with me. Everyone abandoned me. May it not be counted against them. ¹⁷ But the Lord stood with me and gave me strength so that I might preach the Good News in its entirety for all the Gentiles to hear. And he rescued me from certain death.[a] ¹⁸ Yes, and the Lord will deliver me from every evil attack and will bring me safely into his heavenly Kingdom. All glory to God forever and ever! Amen. 2 Timothy 4:15 (NLT) Bible Gateway*

Paul, a great missionary did two letters to Timothy with warnings and take responsibility to encourage the people of God. Some leaders are weak in faith, unable to withstand evil attacks that might suddenly occur for lack of teaching and strength of encouragement from other disciples. Disciples will experience trials and tribulations learning through their faith, God will rescue them and expect them to witness to others the Glory of deliverance.

- ¹¹ Now these are the gifts Christ gave to the church: the apostles, the prophets, the evangelists, and the pastors and teachers. *Ephesians 4:11 (NLT) Bible Gateway*

Paul is speaking to the Church of Ephesus that God gives a "calling" with various gifting for disciples to receive knowledge to serve Him in an FBO having Christian education as the foundation to edify others.

The Bible commands with directives for FBO to obediently follow and implement for the body of believers to receive Christian education for developing spiritual growth. Christian Education has been a benchmark for FBOs for centuries in some cities i.e. New York City, (former residence) experiencing two FBOs as educational sites for discipleship teaching and training at no cost to individuals receiving certificates. The local church would additionally have "called" Christian educators, leaders of a ministry, and individuals using their talents rendering service to the FBO constituents. As servant of Christian Education ministry, teachers were perpetually receiving teaching and training with preparedness to serve up to the highest level of age within the FBO. The Christian education ministry is the foundation of the FBOs over centuries with fortitude for knowledge and growth of disciples birthing spiritual gifting leaders.

Unfortunately, revisiting New York City, Christian Education has become obsolete with upcoming young senior pastors viewing it as unimportant inclusive of Sunday school session and teaching sessions believing preaching to be the catalyst for spiritual growth.

The inception of new membership orientation for FBOs under Christian education for baptism orientation of new disciples and after baptism with additional sessions for purpose of serving is declining in New York City and other outlying vicinities in the Northeastern corridor of FBOs. Christian education is also plummeting in the southern corridor of FBOs that is most discouraging. Following baptism, some FBOS are in preparedness for new disciples after welcoming into the FBO to give an assignment of classes to learn doctrine of faith, stewardship, spiritual gifts, Life of Christ, introduction to the life of the FBO and active ministries. Disciples of all ages following sessions of teaching/training from the Christian educator's sessions can serve using one of their options: speak, sing, teach, serve as missionaries, serve youth, or become leader of a ministry. Prayerfully, the Holy Spirit will move using anointing servants to avert FBO leader's declination to resumption of Christian education according to the will of God to "feed his sheep" and children inclusively.

## "What About The Children (Lambs)"?

Tavis Smiley's question to the Jamestown 400th Anniversary held at Hampton University in February 2007 for his book, "The Covenant" having several panelists. The panelist's discussion during the session gave a threading of "what about the children" that are exhibiting many issues that could use school, families, community and church assistance. Should these paradigms actively develop teaching and mentoring sessions to heal and improve the lives of children, children could mature becoming productive adults. As an attendee, Tavis gave recognition the audience represents the church, possibly referencing that during daily commuting, individuals have the opportunity to minister to children they might encounter.

Taking another perspective concern for the life of children, the story of "creation: could save many if FBOs had Sunday school and discipleship classes.

*As a teenager, the "Creation Story" Sunday school lesson spoke into this author's life not liking self with low self-esteem having a dynamic teacher, receiving continuous Christian educational knowledge through teaching did grow into servant leadership.*

Leaders that should be servant leaders would know it is imperative to teach and develop children ministry to prepare future servants for the FBOs to maintain continuous stronghold. Unfortunately, children are developing with history of childhood abuse requiring nurturing for healing to become leaders of tomorrow. Until there is transformation of leaders to servant leader FBO are unable to have spiritual discernment of resuming Christian education for strengthening disciples of all ages that is inclusive of children.

*5 And now, a word to you who are elders in the churches. I, too, am an elder and a witness to the sufferings of Christ. And I, too, will share in his glory when he is revealed to the whole world. As a fellow elder, I appeal to you: ² Care for the flock that God has entrusted to you. Watch over it willingly, not grudgingly—not for what you will get out of it, but because you are eager to serve God. ³ Don't lord it over the people assigned to your care, but lead them by your own good example. 1Peter 5:1-3 (NLT) Bible Gateway*

Peter is speaking to pastors shepherding the worship attendees having the expectation to receive Christian educational knowledge with servant leaders neglecting their assignment of God desiring his sheep to grow from shepherds feeding his flock. Pastors are exhibiting their own mindset in the decision making of feeding the flock by disqualifying Christian studies believing their way is acceptable.

*The FBOs should resume its assignment with servant leaders and obey the Great Commission, Matthew 28:19-20 through Christian educators structuring perpetual discipleship classes for continuous growth for a relationship with God.*

Leaders are shifting the Word of God but servant leaders are to obey the Great Commission to make disciples according to Matthew 28:19-20. This author is obedient to provoke leaders of FBOs to change behaviors by transformation, as there is not much time God will grant another opportunity.

## The Lamb and Sheep

Lambs are infants, youth, young adults, adults, senior citizens representing genealogy of life for families and church requiring nurturing or become extinct. The extinction of family life can be devastating if individuals lack knowledge they are losing the "gift of salvation" that is free for all to receive if Christian education is active. Realistically, FBOs disqualifying Christian education is a deliberate starvation to the body of believers at all ages. FBOs are oblivious that Christian education can starve lambs if they only drink milk and not able to increase their knowledge of the Word. It is probable that many FBOs without Christian education have lambs drinking milk with some lambs and sheep still unable to swallow meat the Word of God, lacking comprehension it is a lifestyle.

There is a serious "cry" for the lambs and sheep that FBOs leaders lack awareness, when lambs and sheep come into the arc of safety it is through the "calling" of an educator for Christian education that would avert returning to the wild. Of special note, not negating the dynamic sermon messages by any means, sermon messages are unable to replace Christian education as it is not sufficient food to feed God's lambs and sheep for lifetime thriving. The Word of God is so full and rich that it solves a multitude of issues psychologically, physically, socially, theologically and personally.

Senior Clergy are responsible for each lamb and sheep that receives membership, baptism, and left by the wayside to find their way and not receive Christian educational classes for continuous knowledge as "They are like Trees planted along the riverbank" Psalm 1:3a, (NLT), Bible Gateway. Psalm of David illustrate trees that could represent lamb and sheep receiving watering of the Word permitting them to flourish and grow becoming servant leaders, without the water, they will die of thirst. To FBO senior clergy, should it be how many thousands we are able to capture for membership quotient or should it be feeding the lamb and sheep nourishment of the Word through teaching and preaching with Christian educational foundation in place for retention of the flock and not let the flock scatter.

## Evangelism, Missions, Ushers, etc

Christian education is imperative for evangelizing the lost, as it is amazing the Jehovah Witnesses evangelize with diligence and commitment whether you are leaving for church, at home not attending a church, or an active member of a church, they accomplish their assignment.

Unfortunately, evangelizing is a simple assignment for all believers of faith as each believer represents the "church". The teaching of this knowledge is through Sunday school teaching and Christian educational teaching, with senior clergy making it obsolete, lamb and sheep are facing starvation of knowledge.

Missions with missionary servants lack knowledge of their assignment as it is more than wearing uniforms and having a special Sunday, the field is plentiful but the laborers are few until they receive adequate teaching to comprehend their true assignment for Kingdom building. This author remembered during her childhood witnessing going to the hospitals, nursing homes as a child with adult chaperons ministering the Word of healing. During this author's young age as a "lamb" able to witness healing of the sick entering the doors of worship, lifting wheelchair bound up steep steps not having elevators, coming to worship. Missionary classes were invaluable to learn the missionary's tasks are for Kingdom building that was a continuation for this author after transitioning to Virginia taking classes at the Baptist General Convention in Richmond for youth and no longer available. There is earlier mention of external sources for the FBO believers to benefit in addition to Christian educational settings within the faith organization that is also waning and unavailable for growing lamb and sheep.

# Discussion

Spiritual to Servant Leadership provide FBOs with options for leadership decision-making, as there are struggles with leaders in specific roles that are influencing the body of believers. The new traits and standards present the opportunity to transform leaders to be followers of Christ taking control with responsibility as a servant leader. Servant leaders are important to prevent spiritual drowsiness that might be cause for long-term spiritual weakening with FBOs disciples.

*[40] Then he returned to the disciples and found them asleep. He said to Peter, "Couldn't you watch with me even one hour? [41] Keep watch and pray, so that you will not give in to temptation. For the spirit is willing, but the body is weak!" Matthew 26:40-41 (NLT) Bible Gateway*

Matthews writes that Christ could not depend upon his disciples to stay awake and be prayerful to avoid temptation, indicating disciples maybe willing, but they are weak that describes the weak traits found on survey with the one hundred participants. The journey as servant and researcher was with relevance of FBOs having apathetic clergy leaders, unaccountable for performance and commitment to Christian education to edify the body of Christ.

General to Spiritual Leadership places the FBOs in another category of decision-making requiring the organization to recognize having general entitlement as to spiritual leadership entitlement is unauthentic for influencing others. A leader that performs in general interrelational activeness with organizational duties can impart an influence to others unauthentically with spiritual qualities. The Greenleaf resource did introduce new constructs for transforming leaders to servant leader for 21st century organizational leadership. The knowledge of Greenleaf being a minister became a profound reference for validating spiritual leadership versus general leadership. His study is a derision of student revolt in 1970 from displeasure of services from the staff employees, giving concern for servants, and not according to titles. Although employment at the university was general duties, Greenleaf's study recognizes ecclesiastic duties are a performance for persons serving in FBO and employment possessing traits and standards. Greenleaf study of 1970 did propose changes from unauthentic employees to servant leaders having ten character traits as values using Kouzes and Posner's (2013) five leadership practices to enhance the performance of leaders. Spiritual leadership is comparable to servant leadership, and not to overlook as obsolete, as its traits are not similar but not the same as servant that represents Christ as ultimate servant leader.

# Conclusion

In conclusion, the research study contains Greenleaf's servant leader theory and the leadership theories of Kouzes and Posner, with support of other theorists. The exploration for types of leaders with comparison to servant leader is improving leadership efficacy in FBOs.

According to the positive results of the current study, 21st century FBOs are not leading with identifiable servant leaders that provide a challenge to introduce new constructs for transforming leaders within FBOs. The researcher's observation implicates CEOs or senior clergy of FBOs are affecting their subordinates in adverse ways. The research results of the study did postulate the probability that nontransparent senior clergy are with a façade that affects FBO followers. Based on the observations, the researcher is recommending new research in the area of FBO senior clergy leaders. A question to consider, Do clergy leaders perform corporately as leaders without a "calling" or are they performing ecclesiastically as leaders with a "calling" influencing weak traits to subordinates? The FBO leadership could benefit from a research study involve individuals who represent subordinate leaders unknowledgeable they should emulate Christ as a servant leader.

Leaders continue to have ethical and moral issues within profit and nonprofit organizations with such issues existing since biblical times. Greenleaf's 1970 study (rev. 2008) supports the current research with Kouzes and Posner (2013b) supporting the leadership field providing the Leadership Practice Inventory Facilitator Guide, with the LPIS survey instrument to evaluate leaders statistically. The LPIS survey is available in their workbook for educators to acquire for Christian education training of leadership in the church.

During exploration, it became perplexing to learn Greenleaf's traits were not of consideration for 21$^{st}$ century servant leadership issues concerning "called" or "uncalled", by other leadership researchers over the decades. Leaders are human, with flaws and imperfections even when attempting to exhibit more Christ-like virtues of servant leadership that would include more forbearance, more empathy, more tolerance and more acceptances of followers. The research imparts a new study of inhibitors for good leadership with hopes of better leadership for FBOs to experience and exhibit under the challenges of the 21$^{st}$ century society. The provoking question for clergy is whether constituents are receiving perpetual discipleship teaching. In closing, Hosea 4:6 (NLT) Bible Gateway says it is your fault Clergy that my people do not know me, you are not teaching my image to influence others, and have an opportunity to employ resources to transform constituents from leaders to servants.

Additional to this text is a study guide that is indispensable for all "believers (inclusive of youth" seeking an assessment for their spiritual gifting and spiritual growth. The guide gives educators in FBOs some essentials that might assist in preparing a teaching format introducing to beginners an awareness of their spiritual assignment. The guide gives enlightenment of information for "believers" to learn of their identity in Christ that Christian educators can inform through teaching.

# References

Greenleaf, R. K. (1970). *The servant as leader.* Cambridge, MA: Center for Applied Studies.

Greenleaf, R. K. (1977). *Servant leadership: A journey into the nature of legitimate power and greatness.* Mahwah, NJ: Paulist Press.

Greenleaf, R. K. (2008). *The servant as leader* (Rev. ed.). Westfield, IN: Greenleaf Center.

Greenleaf, R. K. (2009). *The institution as servant* (Rev. ed.). Westfield, IN: Greenleaf Center.

Holy Bible. New Living Translation copyright© 1996, 2004, 2007, 2013 by Tyndale House Foundation. Used by permission of Tyndale House Publishers Inc., Carol Stream, Illinois 60188. All rights reserved.

Kouzes, J. M., & Posner, B. Z. (2004). *Christian reflections on leadership challenge.* San Francisco, CA: Jossey-Bass.

Kouzes, J. M. & Posner, B. Z. (2007). *The leadership challenge* (4th ed.). San Francisco, CA: Jossey-Bass.

Kouzes, J. M., & Posner, B. Z. (2013a). *LPI: Leadership practices inventory: Facilitator's guide* (4th ed.). San Francisco, CA: Pfeiffer.

Kouzes, J. M., & Posner, B. Z. (2013b). *LPI: Leadership practices inventory: Self* (4th ed.). San Francisco, CA: Pfeffer.

Printed in the United States
By Bookmasters